Sourdough Cookbook Easy Guide for Beginners

Benefits of Baking Sourdough

By

Parlan Osian
Copyright@2023

Table of Contents

CHAPTER 1 5

Introduction.................................5

   1.1 What is Sourdough? 5

   1.2 Why Make Sourdough at Home? 6

   1.3 Benefits of Baking Sourdough ...8

CHAPTER 2 11

Getting Started with Sourdough 11

   2.1 Essential Ingredients................11

   2.2 Tools and Equipment...............13

   2.3 Understanding the Sourdough Process...16

CHAPTER 3 20

Creating Your Starter........................20

   3.1 What is a Starter?......................20

   3.2 Step-by-Step Guide to Making Your Starter 21

3.3 Troubleshooting Common Starter Issues 23

CHAPTER 4 26

Basic Sourdough Recipes 26

   4.1 Classic Sourdough Bread 26

   4.2 Sourdough Pancakes 30

   4.3 Sourdough Pizza Crust 35

CHAPTER 5 41

Advanced Sourdough Techniques 41

   5.1 Shaping and Scoring 41

   5.2 Adding Flavors and Mix-ins 48

   5.3 Experimenting with Different Flours 54

CHAPTER 6 61

Troubleshooting and Tips 61

   6.1 Common Issues and How to Fix Them 61

   6.2 Tips for Perfect Sourdough Every Time 69

CHAPTER 7 77

Sourdough in Your Daily Life 77

   7.1 Incorporating Sourdough into Meals 77

   7.2 Storing and Freezing Sourdough 83

CHAPTER 1

Introduction

1.1 What is Sourdough?

Sourdough is a time-honored method of bread-making that traces its roots back centuries. At its essence, sourdough is a type of bread leavened by naturally occurring wild yeast and lactic acid bacteria. Unlike commercial yeast, which is a single strain cultivated for uniformity, the wild yeast in sourdough comes from the environment, adding a unique character and depth of flavor to the bread.

This ancient fermentation process involves combining flour and water to create a mixture known as the "starter" or "levain." The starter captures wild yeast and bacteria from the surrounding environment, initiating the fermentation that gives sourdough its distinctive taste and texture. This artisanal approach to bread-making not only imparts a nuanced flavor profile but also offers a connection to traditional methods that predate modern industrial baking.

1.2 Why Make Sourdough at Home?

Baking sourdough at home is a deeply rewarding culinary journey that extends beyond the satisfaction of creating a loaf of bread from scratch. There's a profound sense of accomplishment in nurturing and maintaining your sourdough starter, watching it bubble and come to life. The hands-on nature of the process provides a therapeutic and meditative experience, offering a welcome respite from the hustle and bustle of modern life.

Home-baked sourdough also allows for complete control over ingredients, making it an excellent choice for those who are mindful of the quality of their food. You can choose organic flours, experiment with various grains, and customize the flavor by adjusting fermentation times and temperatures. This level of control empowers bakers to create a loaf that not only suits their taste preferences but also aligns with dietary choices and restrictions.

The act of making sourdough fosters a connection to the broader food community. Sharing sourdough with friends and family becomes a gesture of warmth and care, a tangible expression of time and effort invested in creating something special. As a result, baking sourdough at home transcends the mere act of preparing food; it becomes a shared experience that strengthens bonds and traditions.

1.3 Benefits of Baking Sourdough

Baking sourdough offers a myriad of benefits that extend beyond the delectable end product. Firstly, sourdough fermentation breaks down gluten and phytic acid, potentially making the bread more digestible for those with sensitivities. The longer fermentation process also contributes to a lower glycemic index, potentially providing more stable blood sugar levels compared to commercially produced bread.

Moreover, the probiotic content in sourdough, courtesy of the lactic acid bacteria, may promote gut health and enhance nutrient absorption. This aligns with a growing awareness of the intimate connection between a healthy gut microbiome and overall well-being.

In addition to its potential health advantages, baking sourdough engages individuals in a continuous learning process. As bakers experiment with different flours, hydration levels, and fermentation times, they hone their skills and develop a nuanced understanding of the art and science of bread-making. This educational aspect not only enriches the baking experience but also fosters a sense of mastery and confidence in the kitchen.

Lastly, the environmental impact of homemade sourdough is worth noting. By eschewing commercially produced bread with its associated packaging and transportation costs, home bakers contribute to a more sustainable and eco-friendly approach to nourishment.

Baking sourdough at home transcends the act of making bread; it becomes a holistic and enriching practice that connects individuals to tradition, community, and a deeper understanding of the food they consume. As we embark on this sourdough journey together, let the joy of discovery and the aroma of freshly baked bread inspire you to explore the world of artisanal baking.

CHAPTER 2

Getting Started with Sourdough

2.1 Essential Ingredients

Embarking on your sourdough journey requires an understanding of the fundamental ingredients that play a pivotal role in crafting this delectable bread.

- **Flour**: Choose high-quality, unbleached flour for the best results. Common choices include all-purpose flour, bread flour, or a combination of whole wheat and white flour to add depth of flavor.

- **Water**: The quality of water is often underestimated. Use filtered or dechlorinated water at room temperature, as excessive chlorine can inhibit the growth of beneficial microbes in your sourdough starter.

- **Salt**: Though a seemingly simple ingredient, salt contributes to the flavor and texture of your sourdough. Opt for a fine sea salt or kosher salt to enhance the overall taste.

- **Sourdough Starter**: This is the heart of sourdough baking. A mixture of flour and water that captures wild yeast and bacteria, a sourdough starter imparts the characteristic tang and leavening power to your bread.

- **Optional Add-ins**: While not strictly necessary, additional ingredients like honey, sugar, or even spices can be incorporated to customize your sourdough's flavor profile.

2.2 Tools and Equipment

Equipping yourself with the right tools is essential for a seamless sourdough baking experience. Here's a comprehensive list to get you started:

- **Mixing Bowls**: Large bowls for mixing and fermenting your dough are essential. Opt for glass or stainless steel to avoid unwanted reactions with the ingredients.

- **Digital Scale**: Precise measurements are crucial in sourdough baking. A digital scale ensures accuracy and consistency, leading to better results.

- **Dough Scraper**: This versatile tool helps in handling sticky dough, shaping, and cleaning surfaces. A bench scraper is invaluable in every sourdough kitchen.

- **Banneton or Proofing Basket**: Shaping your dough and allowing it to rise properly is aided by a banneton. These baskets create a beautiful pattern on the crust and help maintain the dough's shape.

- **Dutch Oven or Bread Cloche**: Achieving a crispy crust and excellent oven spring is simplified with a covered baking vessel. A Dutch oven or bread cloche traps steam during baking, mimicking professional bread ovens.

- **Lame or Razor Blade**: Scoring your dough before baking allows it to expand properly. A sharp lame or razor blade helps create intricate patterns on the crust.

- **Kitchen Towels and Linen Couche**: These are used for covering your rising dough and promoting proper fermentation. A linen couche aids in shaping long or baguette-style loaves.

- **Thermometer**: Monitoring dough and water temperatures ensures optimal conditions for fermentation. Precision is key in maintaining a healthy sourdough culture.

Investing in quality tools enhances your baking experience and contributes to the overall success of your sourdough endeavors.

2.3 Understanding the Sourdough Process

Delving into the intricacies of the sourdough process is essential for honing your baking skills. The journey from creating a starter to baking a flavorful loaf involves several key steps:

- **Creating a Sourdough Starter**: Begin by combining equal parts flour and water and allowing the mixture to ferment. Regular feeding cultivates a robust community of wild yeast and bacteria.

- **Feeding and Maintaining the Starter**: Regular feeding keeps your starter healthy and active. Understanding the signs of a well-fed starter, such as a bubbly appearance and a pleasant aroma, is crucial.

- **Autolyse**: Allowing the flour and water to rest before incorporating the salt and starter improves gluten development and enhances the final texture of your bread.

- **Bulk Fermentation**: The initial rise of the dough occurs during bulk fermentation. Folding the dough at intervals strengthens the gluten structure and develops flavor.

- **Shaping**: Pre-shaping and final shaping contribute to the loaf's structure and appearance. A well-shaped loaf translates to a beautifully risen final product.

- **Proofing**: Allowing the shaped dough to undergo its final rise is a critical step. This ensures a light and airy crumb in the finished bread.

- **Scoring**: Before baking, scoring the dough controls its expansion and influences the final appearance. It also enhances the texture of the crust.

- **Baking**: A hot oven, preheated vessel, and steam are essential for achieving a crispy crust and an open crumb. Understanding your oven's nuances is key to mastering the baking process.

- **Cooling**: Allowing the bread to cool completely before slicing is crucial for the texture and flavor to fully develop.

Comprehending each stage of the sourdough process, you gain the knowledge needed to troubleshoot, experiment, and ultimately master the art of sourdough baking.

CHAPTER 3

Creating Your Starter

3.1 What is a Starter?

A sourdough starter is a live culture of wild yeast and lactic acid bacteria that ferments a mixture of flour and water. It serves as the leavening agent for sourdough bread, imparting the characteristic tang and contributing to a well-developed crumb. The starter is a symbiotic community of microorganisms, and its cultivation involves creating an environment conducive to the growth of both yeast and bacteria. As the starter matures, it becomes a reliable and flavorful foundation for your sourdough recipes.

3.2 Step-by-Step Guide to Making Your Starter

Creating a sourdough starter is a rewarding process that requires patience and precision. Follow these steps for a successful starter:

Ingredients:

- 1 cup all-purpose flour (whole wheat or a mix can be used for added nutrients)
- 1/2 to 3/4 cup room temperature, dechlorinated water

Day 1: In a glass or plastic container, mix 1/2 cup of flour with enough water to create a thick but pourable consistency. Cover loosely with a cloth or plastic wrap.

Day 2: Check for any signs of bubbles or fermentation. If none are present, discard half of the mixture and add equal parts flour and water, stirring until smooth. Cover again.

Day 3: By now, you may notice bubbles and a slightly tangy aroma. Discard half of the mixture and feed it as on Day 2. Repeat daily.

Days 4-7: Continue discarding and feeding daily until the starter doubles in size within 4-6 hours of feeding. It should have a pleasant, tangy aroma and display vigorous bubbles.

Maintenance (After 7 Days): Once your starter is active, you can refrigerate it and feed it once a week, bringing it to room temperature and discarding and feeding as before.

Note: The time it takes to develop a starter may vary based on environmental factors, so use visual cues and aroma as indicators of readiness.

3.3 Troubleshooting Common Starter Issues

Even with careful attention, you might encounter challenges in the starter creation process. Here are common issues and solutions:

- **No Bubbles or Rise:**
  - *Solution:* Ensure proper temperature (ideally 70-75°F or 21-24°C), and be patient. If there's still no activity after a week, consider adjusting the flour-to-water ratio or changing the type of flour.

- **Unpleasant Smell (Not Tangy):**
  - *Solution:* A strong, unpleasant odor might indicate harmful bacteria. Restart the process with clean utensils and containers, and use a higher hydration ratio to favor yeast over undesirable microbes.

- **Mold Growth:**
  - *Solution:* Discard the affected portion immediately. Ensure proper hygiene, use clean containers, and consider reducing the hydration level to make the environment less favorable for mold.

- **Slow Development:**
  - *Solution:* If your starter is taking longer to mature, maintain a consistent feeding schedule, and consider adjusting the temperature. A warmer environment encourages microbial activity.

understanding the nuances of creating and troubleshooting a sourdough starter, you pave the way for successful and flavorful bread-making endeavors.

CHAPTER 4

Basic Sourdough Recipes

4.1 Classic Sourdough Bread

Baking a classic sourdough bread is a gratifying experience, and the following recipe provides a step-by-step guide for beginners:

Ingredients:

- 1 cup active sourdough starter
- 1 1/2 cups lukewarm water
- 4 cups bread flour
- 1 1/2 teaspoons salt

Instructions:

Day 1: Mixing the Dough

1. **Feed Your Starter:** Ensure your sourdough starter is active and has been fed within the last 4-8 hours.

2. **Combine Ingredients:** In a large mixing bowl, combine the active starter and lukewarm water. Stir until well mixed.

3. **Add Flour:** Gradually add the bread flour to the mixture, stirring continuously. Once a shaggy dough forms, let it rest for 30 minutes. This period is known as autolyse, enhancing gluten development.

4. **Incorporate Salt:** Sprinkle salt over the dough and fold it in, ensuring even distribution. Cover the bowl and let it rest.

Day 1: Bulk Fermentation

5. **Folding:** Perform a series of folds every 30 minutes for the first 2 hours. Wet your hands to prevent sticking. Afterward, let the dough rest, covered, for an additional 2-4 hours or until it has doubled in size.

Day 1: Shaping and Proofing

6. **Pre-shape:** Turn the dough out onto a floured surface and gently pre-shape it into a round. Let it rest for 20-30 minutes.

7. **Final Shape:** Shape the dough into its final form, either a round or oval. Place it in a floured banneton or proofing basket, seam side down.

8. **Final Proof:** Cover the shaped dough and let it proof at room

temperature for 1-2 hours, or until it passes the "poke test" – an indentation made with your finger springs back slowly.

Baking

9. **Preheat Oven:** Preheat your oven to 450°F (232°C) with a Dutch oven inside.

10. **Score the Dough:** Carefully score the top of your proofed dough with a sharp knife or lame.

11. **Bake:** Place the dough, still in the proofing basket, into the preheated Dutch oven. Cover and bake for 20 minutes. Uncover and continue baking for an additional 20-25 minutes or until the crust is golden brown.

12. **Cooling:** Allow the bread to cool on a wire rack for at least an hour before slicing.

Enjoy the satisfaction of slicing into your homemade classic sourdough bread, with its chewy crust and airy crumb, revealing the distinctive flavor that only a well-crafted sourdough can provide.

4.2 Sourdough Pancakes

Sourdough pancakes are a delightful way to repurpose excess sourdough starter and infuse breakfast with a tangy twist. Here's a straightforward recipe for scrumptious sourdough pancakes:

Ingredients:

- 1 cup active sourdough starter

- 1 cup all-purpose flour
- 1 cup milk (dairy or plant-based)
- 1 large egg
- 2 tablespoons melted butter or oil
- 2 tablespoons sugar
- 1 teaspoon baking soda
- 1/2 teaspoon salt
- Optional: vanilla extract, cinnamon, or fruit for added flavor

Instructions:

1. **Prepare the Sourdough Starter:**
    - Ensure your sourdough starter is active and has been recently fed.

2. **Mix the Wet Ingredients:**

    - In a large mixing bowl, whisk together the active sourdough starter, milk, egg, and melted butter or oil until well combined.

3. **Incorporate Dry Ingredients:**

    - Add the flour, sugar, baking soda, and salt to the wet ingredients. Mix until just combined, being careful not to overmix. If desired, add a splash of vanilla extract or sprinkle in some cinnamon for extra flavor.

4. **Rest the Batter:**

    - Let the batter rest for about 10-15 minutes.

This allows the sourdough to interact with the other ingredients and enhances the pancake's texture.

5. **Preheat the Griddle or Pan:**

    - Preheat a griddle or non-stick pan over medium heat. Lightly grease the surface with butter or cooking spray.

6. **Cook the Pancakes:**

    - Pour 1/4 cup portions of batter onto the griddle for each pancake. Cook until bubbles form on the surface, then flip and cook the other side until golden brown.

7. **Repeat:**

- Continue cooking the remaining batter in batches, adjusting the heat if needed. Keep cooked pancakes warm in a low oven while you finish the rest.

8. **Serve:**

    - Serve the pancakes warm with your favorite toppings, such as maple syrup, fresh fruit, or a dollop of yogurt.

Tips:

- For extra fluffiness, you can let the batter sit overnight in the refrigerator before cooking.

- Experiment with different flavor additions, such as

blueberries, chocolate chips, or chopped nuts.

These sourdough pancakes offer a unique twist to a classic breakfast favorite, with the tangy flavor of sourdough adding depth and character to each delightful bite.

4.3 Sourdough Pizza Crust

Transform your pizza night with a sourdough-infused crust that adds a delightful tang to every slice. Follow this simple recipe to create a flavorful sourdough pizza crust:

Ingredients:

For the Sourdough Pizza Dough:

- 1 cup active sourdough starter
- 1 cup all-purpose flour

- 1/4 cup olive oil
- 1 teaspoon salt
- 1 teaspoon sugar
- 1/3 cup lukewarm water

For Topping (Customize as Desired):

- Tomato sauce
- Mozzarella cheese
- Fresh vegetables (e.g., bell peppers, tomatoes, mushrooms)
- Pepperoni or your favorite protein
- Fresh herbs (e.g., basil, oregano)

Instructions:

1. Prepare the Sourdough Pizza Dough:

a. In a large bowl, combine the active sourdough starter, all-purpose flour, olive oil, salt, and sugar.

b. Gradually add lukewarm water to the mixture, stirring continuously until a dough forms.

c. Knead the dough on a floured surface for about 5-7 minutes until it becomes smooth and elastic.

d. Place the dough back into the bowl, cover with a damp cloth, and let it rest at room temperature for at least 4 hours or until it doubles in size.

2. Preheat the Oven:

- Preheat your oven to the highest temperature it can reach (usually around 475-500°F or 245-260°C). If you have a pizza stone, place it in the oven during the preheating.

3. Shape the Pizza Dough:

a. Punch down the risen dough and transfer it to a floured surface.

b. Roll out the dough into your desired pizza shape and thickness.

4. Assemble the Pizza:

a. If you have a pizza peel, transfer the rolled-out dough onto it. If not, use a piece of parchment paper on a baking sheet.

b. Spread tomato sauce evenly over the dough, leaving a border for the crust.

c. Add your favorite toppings, such as cheese, vegetables, and proteins.

5. Bake the Pizza:

- If using a pizza stone, carefully transfer the pizza (on the parchment paper) onto the hot stone in the oven. If not using a stone, simply place the baking sheet in the oven.

- Bake for 12-15 minutes or until the crust is golden brown, and the cheese is melted and bubbly.

6. Serve and Enjoy:

- Remove the pizza from the oven, let it cool for a few minutes, slice, and serve.

Tips:

- Experiment with different cheeses and toppings to create your favorite flavor combinations.

- For a crispier crust, pre-bake the rolled-out dough for a few minutes before adding toppings.

This sourdough pizza crust recipe adds a delightful twist to your homemade pizza, making it a flavorful and unique experience for your taste buds.

CHAPTER 5

Advanced Sourdough Techniques

5.1 Shaping and Scoring

Mastering the art of shaping and scoring is the key to achieving a professional-looking and artisanal sourdough loaf. These advanced techniques contribute not only to the bread's aesthetic appeal but also to its texture and flavor. Here's a detailed guide on how to elevate your sourdough game through effective shaping and scoring:

Shaping:

1. **Pre-shaping:**

- After the bulk fermentation, turn the dough out onto a lightly floured surface.

- Gently fold the edges of the dough toward the center, creating a round shape.

- Allow the dough to rest for 15-30 minutes to relax gluten and make the final shaping easier.

2. **Final Shaping:**

    - Flip the dough over so that the seam is facing down.

    - Create tension on the surface by folding the edges up and toward the center, forming a tight ball.

- For an oval loaf, elongate the ball by gently rolling it back and forth.

3. **Bench Rest:**

    - Place the shaped dough seam-side down and let it bench rest for 15-30 minutes. This allows the gluten to relax slightly and makes scoring more effective.

4. **Transfer to Proofing Basket:**

    - Place the shaped dough into a floured banneton or proofing basket, seam-side up.

Scoring:

1. **Tools:**
   - Use a sharp blade or lame for scoring. A lame allows for precise and controlled cuts.

2. **Technique:**
   - Hold the blade at a 45-degree angle to the surface of the dough.
   - Make swift, confident cuts about 1/4 to 1/2 inch deep. Shallow cuts may close up during baking, while deep cuts can deflate the dough.

3. **Scoring Patterns:**
   - Experiment with different scoring patterns. A simple "X" or a few diagonal slashes

work well for round loaves, while a lengthwise slash suit oval loaf.

- For artistic flair, try geometric patterns or a tic-tac-toe grid.

4. **Depth and Angle:**

    - The depth of the cut affects the degree of expansion during baking. Deeper cuts allow the dough to open up and create an appealing "ear."

    - Vary the angle of your cuts to influence the direction of expansion.

5. **Practice Patience:**

    - Scoring is best done swiftly to prevent

dragging and tearing. Practice on parchment paper to refine your technique.

Baking:

1. **Preheat Oven:**
   - Preheat your oven with a Dutch oven or baking stone inside to create a steamy environment, crucial for optimal oven spring.

2. **Baking with Steam:**
   - Transfer the scored dough, along with the parchment paper, into the preheated Dutch oven or onto the baking stone.
   - Cover with the lid or use a steam-generating

method for the first 20 minutes of baking.

3. **Uncover and Finish Baking:**

   - After the initial steam phase, uncover the dough and continue baking until the desired color is achieved. This typically takes an additional 20-25 minutes.

Cooling and Enjoyment:

1. **Cooling:**

   - Allow the baked bread to cool completely on a wire rack before slicing. This ensures the interior structure sets properly.

2. **Savor the Fruits of Your Labor:**

- Finally, savor the aroma, texture, and flavor of your expertly shaped and scored sourdough masterpiece.

Refining your shaping and scoring techniques, you'll enhance both the visual appeal and taste of your sourdough creations, taking your baking skills to the next level.

5.2 Adding Flavors and Mix-ins

Elevate your sourdough game by exploring the world of flavors and mix-ins. While classic sourdough is a culinary delight on its own, incorporating additional ingredients can introduce new dimensions and exciting taste profiles. Here's a guide on how to expertly add flavors and mix-ins to your sourdough bread:

1. **Selecting Flavors:**

   - Choose complementary flavors that enhance the natural tang of sourdough. Popular options include:

     - **Herbs:** Rosemary, thyme, or oregano add aromatic depth.

     - **Cheese:** Sharp cheeses like cheddar or parmesan bring a savory kick.

     - **Nuts:** Walnuts or pecans provide a delightful crunch.

     - **Seeds:** Sunflower, flax, or pumpkin seeds introduce texture.

- **Dried Fruits:** Apricots, cranberries, or raisins for a touch of sweetness.

2. **Preparation:**

    - For dried fruits or nuts, soak them in warm water or juice before incorporating to prevent them from drawing moisture from the dough during baking.

    - Grate or finely chop hard cheeses to ensure even distribution.

3. **Adding to the Dough:**

    - During the final stages of mixing or folding, gently incorporate your chosen flavors or mix-ins into the dough.

    - For even distribution, fold the dough a few times, allowing the ingredients to be evenly dispersed.

4. **Consider Hydration:**
   - Flavors like seeds or dried fruits may affect the hydration of your dough. Adjust water content accordingly to maintain the desired consistency.

5. **Experiment with Seasonings:**
   - Enhance the overall flavor by experimenting with seasonings. Garlic powder, onion powder, or even a dash of cayenne can add a savory kick.

6. **Layered Flavors:**
   - Experiment with layered flavors by incorporating ingredients at different stages. For example, add fresh herbs

during shaping for a burst of aroma.

7. **Customizing for Sweet or Savory:**

- Customize your sourdough to match your preference. For a sweet twist, consider cinnamon and sugar swirls or chocolate chunks. For a savory option, sun-dried tomatoes and olives can be excellent choices.

8. **Balancing Act:**

- Strive for a balance between your additional ingredients and the inherent flavors of sourdough. The goal is to enhance, not overpower, the classic taste.

9. **Adjusting Fermentation Time:**

- The presence of additional ingredients can impact fermentation. Monitor the dough closely, as certain elements may accelerate or slow down the process.

10. **Baking Considerations:**

    - Note that ingredients like sugar or honey can affect the crust's color due to caramelization during baking.

11. **Shape Creatively:**

    - Consider creative shaping techniques to highlight the added ingredients. For example, create a swirl for cinnamon-sugar or a layered effect for cheese and herbs.

12. **Share and Gather Feedback:**

- Once baked, share your uniquely flavored sourdough and gather feedback. Adjust quantities or combinations based on taste preferences.

Incorporating a variety of flavors and mix-ins, you'll transform your sourdough into a culinary canvas, ready to delight your taste buds with each new batch. Experiment, be creative, and enjoy the journey of crafting personalized sourdough masterpieces.

5.3 Experimenting with Different Flours

Dive into the realm of sourdough alchemy by experimenting with a variety of flours. Each flour brings its own unique flavor, texture, and nutritional profile to your sourdough bread. Here's a comprehensive guide to help you explore the world of different flours in your sourdough baking:

1. **Selecting Alternative Flours:**

    - **Whole Wheat Flour:** Adds a nutty flavor and boosts nutritional content with bran and germ.

    - **Rye Flour:** Imparts a distinct earthy taste and can enhance the sourness of the bread.

    - **Spelt Flour:** Offers a mild, slightly sweet flavor and a unique texture.

    - **Einkorn Flour:** Known for its ancient heritage, it contributes a delicate, nutty taste.

- **Buckwheat Flour:** Introduces a rich, robust flavor and a denser texture.

2. **Blending Flours:**

    - Combine different flours to create a custom blend. For example, a mix of whole wheat and bread flour can yield a flavorful yet well-structured loaf.

3. **Hydration Adjustment:**

    - Different flours absorb water differently. Adjust the hydration level of your dough based on the flour used to achieve the desired consistency.

4. **Experimenting with Ratios:**

    - Start by substituting a portion of your regular flour with an alternative flour. As you become familiar with its characteristics, you can adjust the ratios to suit your taste.

5. **Incorporating Ancient Grains:**

- Experiment with ancient grains like kamut, spelt, or einkorn to add unique flavors and nutritional benefits.

6. **Starter Adaptation:**

- Your sourdough starter can adapt to different flours over time. Feed it consistently with the flour you want to incorporate to encourage the development of the desired microbial community.

7. **Fermentation Variations:**

- Different flours may impact fermentation times. Be attentive to the dough's rise and adjust accordingly.

8. **Maintaining Gluten Structure:**

- Flours with lower gluten content, such as rye, may result in a more delicate crumb. Experiment with additional folds during bulk fermentation to enhance structure.

9. **Flour Combinations:**

- Craft unique combinations like a blend of whole wheat, rye, and spelt for a complex flavor profile.

10. **Savor the Differences:**

- Taste and document the variations in flavor, texture, and aroma introduced by each flour. This experimentation process is a journey of discovery.

11. **Storing Alternative Flours:**

    - Some alternative flours have shorter shelf lives due to higher oil content. Store them in airtight containers in a cool, dark place or the refrigerator to maintain freshness.

12. **Creative Additions:**

    - Combine alternative flours with other creative additions like seeds, nuts, or dried fruits for a multi-dimensional bread.

13. **Community Feedback:**

    - Share your experiments with the sourdough community and gather insights. Others' experiences can provide valuable guidance for future experiments.

Embrace the world of diverse flours as you embark on your sourdough exploration. Each batch becomes an opportunity to create a unique bread with flavors and characteristics that reflect your personal preferences and culinary creativity.

CHAPTER 6

Troubleshooting and Tips

6.1 Common Issues and How to Fix Them

Sourdough baking is both an art and a science, and even seasoned bakers encounter challenges. Here's a troubleshooting guide to help you identify common issues and provide solutions to ensure your sourdough success:

1. Problem: **Dense or Flat Loaf**

- **Solution:**
  - *Possible Cause:* Insufficient fermentation or overproofing.
  - *Fix:* Adjust fermentation times. Perform the "poke test" to gauge proofing. If the indentation springs back slowly, it's ready.

2. Problem: **Lack of Oven Spring**

- **Solution:**
  - *Possible Cause:* Underproofed or overproofed dough.
  - *Fix:* Ensure proper proofing. If your dough hasn't risen adequately, it may lack the strength for a good oven spring.

3. Problem: **Gummy or Wet Crumb**

- **Solution:**

  - *Possible Cause:* Underbaking or high hydration.

  - *Fix:* Extend baking time if the center is gummy. Adjust hydration if the dough is overly wet; reduce water or increase flour.

4. Problem: **Excessive Sourness**

- **Solution:**

  - *Possible Cause:* Prolonged fermentation or high percentage of whole grain flour.

  - *Fix:* Shorten fermentation time or

reduce the amount of whole grain flour for a milder flavor.

5. Problem: **Sticky Dough**

- **Solution:**
  - *Possible Cause:* High hydration or insufficient flour.
  - *Fix:* Adjust hydration levels by adding more flour during mixing or folding.

6. Problem: **Burnt Crust**

- **Solution:**
  - *Possible Cause:* Oven temperature too high.
  - *Fix:* Lower the oven temperature or reduce baking time. Consider

covering the loaf with foil after achieving the desired crust color.

7. Problem: **Weak Gluten Structure**

- **Solution:**
  - *Possible Cause:* Insufficient kneading or folding.
  - *Fix:* Increase the number of folds during bulk fermentation or incorporate a longer autolyse period.

8. Problem: **Unevenly Shaped Loaf**

- **Solution:**
  - *Possible Cause:* Inadequate pre-shaping or shaping.

- *Fix:* Practice proper pre-shaping and shaping techniques, ensuring an even tension on the surface.

9. Problem: **Starter Issues**

- **Solution:**
    - *Possible Cause:* Inactive or weak starter.
    - *Fix:* Revive your starter by feeding regularly, adjusting the ratio of flour to water, or changing the type of flour used.

10. Problem: **Sourdough Starter Separation**

Solution: - *Possible Cause:* Lack of regular feeding. - *Fix:* Discard a portion of the starter and feed it consistently. Maintain a regular feeding schedule.

11. Problem: **Excessive Crust Hardness**

Solution: - *Possible Cause:* High oven temperature or extended baking. - *Fix:* Reduce the oven temperature or shorten the baking time. Monitor the crust's color and adjust accordingly.

12. Problem: **Overly Tangy Flavor**

Solution: - *Possible Cause:* Extended fermentation or high starter percentage. - *Fix:* Shorten fermentation times or reduce the amount of starter used in the recipe.

Tips:

1. **Consistency is Key:**

- Maintain consistent techniques, temperatures, and feeding schedules for both the starter and the dough.

2. **Use a Kitchen Scale:**

    - Precise measurements contribute to consistent results. Weigh ingredients for accuracy.

3. **Experiment Gradually:**

    - When troubleshooting, make one change at a time to identify the specific factor affecting your results.

4. **Document Your Process:**

    - Keep a sourdough journal to track your experiments, noting key details like fermentation times, temperatures, and ingredient ratios.

5. **Join Sourdough Communities:**

    - Engage with online forums or local baking groups to seek advice and share experiences.

sourdough baking is a journey of continuous learning. Embrace challenges, celebrate successes, and refine your techniques as you embark on the path to becoming a seasoned sourdough artisan.

6.2 Tips for Perfect Sourdough Every Time

Achieving the perfect sourdough can be a nuanced and rewarding endeavor.

From cultivating a robust starter to mastering the intricacies of fermentation and baking, here's a comprehensive guide with a multitude of tips to help you consistently produce impeccable sourdough bread:

1. **Starter Maintenance:**

   - *Consistent Feeding:* Establish a regular feeding schedule for your sourdough starter, ideally every 12 hours. This ensures a healthy, active culture.

2. **Hydration Awareness:**

   - *Precise Measurement:* Use a kitchen scale to measure flour and water accurately. This level of precision contributes to a consistent dough texture.

3. **Temperature Control:**

- *Optimal Range:* Maintain a controlled environment for your starter and dough. Ideal fermentation temperatures range between 70-75°F (21-24°C) to foster a balanced and flavorful sourdough.

4. **Autolyse Technique:**

    - *Enhanced Gluten Development:* Incorporate an autolyse step by allowing flour and water to rest before adding the starter and salt. This promotes improved gluten structure and a better-textured crumb.

5. **Customized Flour Blends:**

    - *Diverse Flavors:* Experiment with different flours and blends to create a unique flavor profile. Whole wheat, rye, and spelt flours can add depth and complexity.

6. **Precision in Starter Use:**

- *Adjustment as Needed:* Tailor the amount of starter used based on factors like room temperature, desired fermentation time, and personal taste preferences.

7. **Fermentation Monitoring:**

- *Visual and Tactile Indicators:* Observe the dough's rise during bulk fermentation and proofing. Utilize the "poke test" to assess the dough's readiness by checking how quickly an indentation springs back.

8. **Scoring Mastery:**

- *Sharp Blades:* Invest in a quality lame or razor blade for clean and precise scoring. Experiment with different patterns to enhance the loaf's visual appeal.

9. **Steam for Oven Spring:**

- *Dutch Oven Magic:* Bake your sourdough in a preheated Dutch oven to trap steam. This creates optimal conditions for a robust oven spring and a crispy crust.

10. **Preheat Rigorously:** - *Hot Start:* Ensure your oven is thoroughly preheated before placing the dough inside. Consistent temperature is crucial for even baking.

11. **Post-Bake Cooling:** - *Complete Development:* Allow the baked bread to cool completely on a wire rack before slicing. This permits the interior structure to set fully and ensures a well-developed flavor.

12. **Practice Patience:** - *Time as an Ingredient:* Sourdough baking is an exercise in patience. Resist the urge to rush through fermentation and proofing stages for a more nuanced and developed flavor.

13. **Adjust for Hydration:** - *Adapt to Flour Variations:* Different flours absorb water differently. Adjust the hydration level of your dough based on the flour used to maintain the desired consistency.

14. **Community Engagement:** - *Learn from Others:* Join sourdough communities online or in your local area. Exchange tips, troubleshoot together, and benefit from the collective knowledge of fellow bakers.

15. **Mindful Documentation:** - *Sourdough Journal:* Keep a detailed

record of each bake. Note the type of flour, hydration levels, fermentation times, and any adjustments made. This helps in refining your technique over time.

16. **Creative Exploration:** - *Flavor Additions:* Don't hesitate to get creative with additions like herbs, seeds, or dried fruits. These elements can elevate your sourdough to new culinary heights.

17. **Continuous Learning:** - *Adaptive Approach:* Embrace a growth mindset, viewing each bake as an opportunity to learn and refine your skills. The journey of perfecting sourdough is ongoing.

Incorporating these tips into your sourdough baking routine will contribute to a consistently exceptional end product. Remember, the pursuit of perfect sourdough is a delightful and ever-evolving journey that combines science, art, and a dash of intuition. Enjoy the process and savor the delicious results.

CHAPTER 7

Sourdough in Your Daily Life

7.1 Incorporating Sourdough into Meals

Sourdough is not just a delightful bread; it's a versatile ingredient that can be seamlessly integrated into various meals throughout your day. From breakfast to dinner, here are creative ways to incorporate sourdough into your daily culinary adventures:

1. **Breakfast Bliss:**

- *Sourdough Toast:* Start your day with a classic. Top toasted sourdough slices with butter, avocado, poached eggs, or your favorite breakfast spreads.

- *Sourdough Pancakes or Waffles:* Transform your morning routine with sourdough-based pancakes or waffles. The tangy flavor adds a delightful twist to this breakfast favorite.

- *Breakfast Sandwiches:* Craft a hearty breakfast sandwich using sliced sourdough. Layer with eggs, cheese, and your choice of breakfast meats for a satisfying start.

2. **Lunch Delights:**

    - *Sourdough Grilled Cheese:* Elevate the classic grilled

cheese sandwich by using slices of your favorite sourdough bread. Add different cheeses, and perhaps a layer of caramelized onions or tomato slices.

- *Sourdough Panini:* Create gourmet panini sandwiches with sourdough as the base. Layer with meats, cheeses, and fresh veggies, then press for a crispy, flavorful lunch.

- *Sourdough Flatbread Pizzas:* Roll out sourdough for a quick and delicious flatbread pizza crust. Top with tomato sauce, cheese, and your preferred toppings for a personalized pizza experience.

3. **Snack Time Magic:**

- *Sourdough Crackers:* Transform discarded sourdough starter into crispy crackers. Mix in herbs or seeds for added flavor. Pair with your favorite dips or cheeses.

- *Sourdough Bruschetta:* Slice and toast sourdough, then top with a mix of diced tomatoes, garlic, basil, and olive oil for a delightful snack or appetizer.

4. **Dinner Extravaganza:**

- *Sourdough Croutons:* Cube stale sourdough and bake with olive oil and seasonings to create crunchy croutons. Perfect for salads or as a soup topping.

- *Sourdough Stuffing:* Upgrade your stuffing recipe by incorporating cubed sourdough.

The tangy notes add depth to the dish, complementing the savory herbs.

- *Sourdough Bread Pudding:* Sweet or savory, sourdough bread pudding is a versatile dinner option. Experiment with ingredients like cheese, vegetables, or fruits.

5. **Dessert Indulgence:**

- *Sourdough Cinnamon Rolls:* Impress your loved ones with freshly baked cinnamon rolls using a sourdough base. The tangy undertones offer a delightful contrast to the sweet filling.

- *Sourdough Dessert Pizza:* Roll out a sweetened sourdough crust and top with a layer of cream cheese frosting and fresh fruit for a unique dessert pizza.

- *Sourdough Chocolate Babka:* Twist layers of chocolate and sourdough dough for a decadent dessert reminiscent of the classic babka.

6. **Beverage Companions:**

- *Sourdough Discard Smoothies:* Utilize sourdough discard in smoothies for added nutrition and a subtle tang. Blend with fruits, yogurt, and a touch of honey.

- *Sourdough-infused Cocktails:* Get creative by incorporating sourdough flavors into your cocktails. Consider using sourdough syrup or incorporating a sourdough-infused spirit.

Whether you're indulging in a leisurely weekend brunch or whipping up a quick weeknight dinner, sourdough can be a versatile and flavorful addition to your daily meals. Explore the endless possibilities and savor the unique character that sourdough brings to each dish.

7.2 Storing and Freezing Sourdough

Preserving the freshness and flavor of your sourdough is essential for an enjoyable culinary experience. Here are guidelines for storing and freezing sourdough to maintain its quality over time:

1. **Storing Fresh Sourdough:**

    - *Bread Box or Bread Bag:* Store fresh, fully cooled sourdough in a bread box or a breathable bread bag. This helps maintain a crisp crust without promoting moisture buildup.

- *Paper Bag:* If you don't have a bread box, placing sourdough in a paper bag can also help maintain the crust's texture while preventing it from becoming overly dry.

- *Cut Side Down:* When storing a partially sliced loaf, place the cut side down on a cutting board or wrapped in beeswax wrap to minimize exposure to air.

2. **Refrigerating Sourdough:**

- *Extended Freshness:* If you don't plan to consume your sourdough within a couple of days, refrigeration can extend its freshness. Wrap the bread in plastic wrap or place it in a plastic bag.

- *Reheating:* To revive refrigerated sourdough, preheat the oven to 350°F (175°C), mist the bread lightly with water, and warm it for about 10 minutes. This restores the crust's crispness.

3. **Freezing Sourdough:**

- *Whole Loaf:* For longer storage, freeze the whole loaf. Double-wrap it in plastic wrap or aluminum foil to prevent freezer burn. Place the wrapped loaf in a freezer-safe bag.

- *Sliced Bread:* If you prefer to freeze individual slices for convenience, place parchment paper between slices to prevent sticking. Wrap the entire batch in plastic wrap and place it in a freezer bag.

4. **Thawing Frozen Sourdough:**

- *Slow Thaw:* To preserve the texture, thaw frozen sourdough gradually. Remove it from the freezer and let it thaw at room temperature or in the refrigerator for a few hours.

- *Oven Revival:* For a crisper crust, preheat the oven to 350°F (175°C), mist the bread lightly with water, and warm it for 10-15 minutes.

5. **Freezing Sourdough Starter:**

- *Dormant Stage:* If you have excess sourdough starter, freeze it in a dormant state. Place a portion in a freezer-safe container and thaw when ready to use.

- *Reviving Frozen Starter:* To revive a frozen starter, thaw it in the refrigerator. Once thawed, feed the starter as you normally would and allow it to become active before using it in your recipes.

6. **Best Practices:**

- *Portion Control:* Consider slicing the loaf before freezing so you can easily thaw and consume only the amount you need.

- *Avoid Refrigeration for Freshness:* While refrigeration can extend shelf life, it may alter the texture. For optimal freshness, consume sourdough within a few days or freeze for longer storage.

- *Quality Check:* Before freezing, ensure your sourdough is fully cooled to room temperature to prevent condensation that could affect its quality in the freezer.

7. **Note on Sourdough Discard:**

- *Freezing Discard:* If you have excess sourdough discard, it can be frozen for later use in recipes like pancakes or waffles. Store it in a freezer-safe container.

Following these storage and freezing guidelines, you can enjoy the delicious taste and texture of your sourdough bread for an extended period, ensuring that every slice remains a delightful culinary experience.

Made in the USA
Columbia, SC
30 June 2025